Brave Maddie Egg

by Natalie Standiford

illustrated by Lynne Woodcock Cravath

A STEPPING STONE BOOK

Random House New York

Library of Congress Cataloging-in-Publication Data
Standiford, Natalie.
Brave Maddie Egg / by Natalie Standiford ; illustrated by Lynne Cravath.
p. cm.
"A Stepping stone book."
SUMMARY: Brave Maddie is secretly afraid of putting her head in the water—a fear
that she must overcome if she wants to go on a boating trip with her family.
ISBN 0-679-85808-3 (pbk.) — ISBN 0-679-95808-8 (lib. bdg.)
[1. Fear—Fiction. 2. Swimming—fiction.] I. Cravath, Lynne Woodcock, ill.
II. Title.
PZ7.S78627Br 1995
[Fic]—dc20
94-29272

Manufactured in the United States of America 10 9 8 7 6 5 4 3 2 1

To my seafaring dad

1

"Bert, where's your bathing suit?" asked Maddie Egg.

Her little brother was running down the hallway with no clothes on.

It was a warm afternoon in June. The Egg family was going to the pool for the first time that summer.

"Bert, I'm hot," Maddie said crossly. She took her four-year-old brother by the hand and started toward his room. Her sister Carrie followed them.

"Stop!" Bert cried. "Don't go in there!"

"Why not?" asked Maddie.

"There's a monster on my bathing suit!" Bert wriggled in horror.

"A monster!" Carrie screamed. She was six. Maddie thought Carrie should know better.

"There's no monster," said Maddie. She walked down the hall to Bert's room. Bert and Carrie followed, clinging to her.

Maddie peeked into the room. It was a mess. Bert's clothes were scattered all over the floor.

"Bert, I don't see any monster," said Maddie.

"It's behind that pile of socks," said Bert. "Next to the dresser."

Something moved in the pile of socks.

"The monster!" screamed Bert and Carrie together.

"What's all this screaming about?" Mrs. Egg stood behind them in the doorway.

"Oh, Mommy," said Bert, clutching his mother's hand. "There's a monster on my bathing suit."

"I'm sure it's not a monster," said Mrs. Egg.

"The socks moved!" cried Carrie.

"I'll see what it is," said Maddie. She marched into the room. Everyone else tiptoed in behind her.

"There it is!" cried Bert. "There's the monster!"

Slithering on top of Bert's bathing suit was a long black snake.

Bert, Carrie, and Mrs. Egg screamed. But Maddie calmly reached down and picked up the snake with her bare hands.

"Put it down, Maddie!" shouted her mother.

"It won't hurt us," said Maddie. "It's just a garden snake." She held it up for everyone to see. Bert, Carrie, and her mother all screamed again.

"Take it outside, Maddie," said her mother. "Quickly." She looked at the snake again and shuddered.

Maddie took the snake outside and left it

in the garden. Then she went back upstairs to Bert's room. Her mother was helping Bert put on his bathing suit.

"Thank you, Maddie," said her mother. "Thank goodness you're so brave."

Maddie *was* brave. Everyone said so.

Maddie brushed her hands together after a job well done. "Now can we please go to the pool?"

The Eggs piled into the steamy-hot car. Maddie was excited. She had just finished second grade, and she was ready for summer.

Summer never really begins, Maddie thought, until I stick my big toe into the pool.

On the way they passed a beat-up red convertible. Its top was down. A young man was driving it. He wore sunglasses and waved.

"Is that Bob?" asked Maddie.

Bob was Bert's invisible friend. Bob was sixteen. He could drive.

"Bob's car is blue," said Bert. "And anyway, he's invisible."

The pool parking lot was nearly full. Maddie walked across the hot gravel in her blue flip-flops. She could hear the shouts of kids playing in the water and the sharp *tweet* of the lifeguard's whistle.

Maddie walked through the entrance gate and down the shady breezeway. Her flip-flops went *thwap-thwap* against her heels. She walked past the damp dressing rooms, past the snack bar, to a patch of grass. There she spread out her towel.

Carrie, Bert, and Mrs. Egg were right behind her. But Maddie didn't wait for them. She walked quickly to the edge of the pool and dipped her big toe in the water.

Summer had begun.

2

Splash!

Bert jumped in at the shallow end. He sank to the bottom and bobbed back up again, laughing.

Carrie jumped in after him, holding her nose. She was careful to keep her head above the water. Bert splashed her. She splashed him back. "Come on, Maddie!" said Carrie.

But Maddie liked to get in slowly. One corner of the pool had four wide steps. Maddie walked down the steps, standing on each one a short time, until the water began to feel warm.

Suddenly a girl popped up beside Maddie. She had been swimming under the water, holding her breath. It was Maddie's friend Emma Doyle.

"Hi, Maddie," said Emma. She shook her wet hair.

"Hi, Emma," said Maddie. "I didn't know you could swim like that."

"I took lessons at the Y this winter," said Emma. "I passed the beginner test. It was a cinch."

"Oh," said Maddie.

"I learned a new game," Emma said. "Want to play?"

"Okay," said Maddie. She stepped down onto the bottom of the pool. The water came up to her chest.

Emma swam along the shallow end, diving under the water like a dolphin. Maddie followed. She bounced from one foot to the other like an astronaut walking on the moon.

She was careful not to get her face wet.

Emma reached over the side of the pool. She held up a shiny penny.

"You toss the penny, and I'll dive down and get it," she said.

Maddie took the penny. "Ready?" she asked. Emma nodded.

Maddie threw the penny into the water. Emma disappeared with a splash. A few seconds later she popped up, the penny in her hand.

"Now you try it," she said.

Splash! Carrie jumped in beside Maddie, holding her nose as always.

"Can I play with you?" she asked.

"No," said Emma. "I think you're too little for this game."

Carrie frowned, but she didn't leave. "I'll watch," she said.

Emma tossed the penny. Maddie watched it sink under the water.

"Go get it," said Emma.

Maddie looked at her. She didn't move.

"What are you waiting for?" Emma asked.

Maddie stared at the spot where the penny went down. She wanted to go underwater and get it. But as soon as she thought about going underwater, something strange happened.

Her heart began to pound.

The blood rushed to her head.

She tried to tell herself not to be afraid. But her ears were ringing. *Riiiing!* Louder and louder.

The ringing blocked out all other sounds. She couldn't hear the lifeguard's whistle. She couldn't hear the kids playing. All she could hear was the terrible ringing in her ears. *Ring! Ring!*

"Yoo-hoo, Maddie," said Emma. She waved her hand in front of Maddie's face.

Maddie's ears cleared. She snapped out of it.

"What's wrong?" Emma asked.

Maddie didn't know what to say. "I think I have water in my ears," she lied.

Emma just shrugged. She dived down, picked up the penny, and came up with it in her hand.

"How do you do that?" Carrie asked Emma. "Can you open your eyes under water?"

Emma nodded. "It's easy. You want to try again, Maddie?"

Maddie shook her head. "Let's play Marco Polo," she said.

"Are you afraid?" Emma asked.

"Maddie's not afraid of anything," said Carrie. "This morning she picked up a huge black snake with her bare hands."

But Carrie was wrong. Maddie *was* afraid of something.

Maddie was afraid to put her head under the water.

3

The lifeguard blew her whistle. Adult swim.

Maddie, Carrie, and Emma got out of the pool and went to the snack bar. Maddie forgot all about the game with the penny. No one asked her to put her head under the water again that day.

That night Mr. Egg brought a pizza home after work. "Hey, kids," he said. "I've got a big surprise!"

"What is it?" asked Maddie.

"What is it? What is it?" Bert said, patting Mr. Egg's pockets.

Mr. Egg kissed Mrs. Egg and set the pizza on the kitchen table. "Sit down and I'll tell you about it," he said.

Maddie passed out plates and Mr. Egg put a slice of pizza on each one.

"It's about our vacation," said Mr. Egg. "We're not going to the beach this year."

"We're not?" said Carrie.

"Why?" asked Maddie.

"Because—" Mr. Egg let the word hang in the air. Maddie and Carrie and Bert sat perfectly still, waiting to hear the reason.

"Because—"

"Because why?" Bert demanded.

"Because—we're going on a boat trip!"

"Hurray!" cried Maddie and Carrie and Bert. They jumped up from the table. Bert ran around it three times. Maddie and Carrie slapped each other five. Mr. and Mrs. Egg laughed.

"We're going to charter a boat with a cabin," said Mrs. Egg. "A boat you can sleep on."

"And we'll sail all around the Chesapeake Bay," said Mr. Egg. "We'll stop at little towns on the shore. We'll explore islands."

"Desert islands?" asked Maddie. She had always wanted to explore a desert island—and maybe find some pirate treasure.

"Sure," said Mr. Egg. "We'll try to find a desert island just for you, Brave Maddie Egg."

"Can we fish off the end of the boat?" asked Carrie.

"You bet," said Mr. Egg.

"Can Bob come, too?" asked Bert.

"There's no room for Bob," Maddie said. "He'll have to ride alongside in his own motorboat."

Bert pouted. "I'm not going if Bob's not going!" he said.

"Don't tease him, Maddie," said Mrs. Egg. "Of course Bob can come with us."

Maddie picked up her slice of pizza and bit into it. A boat trip! It sounded exciting.

"We'll go the first week of August," said Mr. Egg. "There's only one condition. Before we go, you each must pass the swimming test for beginners."

Maddie spit out her pizza.

"A boat can be very dangerous," said Mrs. Egg. "If you fall overboard, you have to know what to do."

"But Dad—" Maddie began.

"No buts," said Mr. Egg. "I won't budge on this. If you want to go sailing, you have to know how to swim. That's final."

"Tomorrow morning you'll all start swimming lessons," said Mrs. Egg.

Not me, thought Maddie. I'm not taking any swimming lessons. I know what swimming lessons *really* mean.

They mean putting your head under water.

4

Early the next morning Mrs. Egg drove the kids to the pool on her way to the hospital. She worked part time as a nurse.

"I'll be back around noon," she called, waving from the car window. "Have fun!"

Bert and Carrie waved cheerfully back at their mother, but Maddie only grumbled, "Have fun yourself."

It was eight o'clock, and the air was still chilly. Swimming lessons start too early in the morning, Maddie thought. I'm supposed to sleep late in the summer. I might as well go to school.

She followed Carrie and Bert through the entrance gate. Her flip-flops *thwap-thwapped,* just as they always did. But this time the sound did not cheer her.

The pool was empty. Maddie could hear the hum of the water filter as she passed the shuttered snack bar.

Seven children had gathered by the shallow end of the pool. Maddie, Carrie, and Bert dropped their towels on the grass and joined them.

Maddie looked around at the other kids. They were all shorter than she was. Most of them were five or six, Carrie's age. Maddie was seven and a half. Her heart sank. She was in the baby group.

She sat down hard on the cold cement, hugging her knees. I knew this was a bad idea, she thought.

One of the lifeguards walked out of the dressing room. A boy of about fifteen joined her. The lifeguard was blond and already tan. She wore a blue tank suit with a lifesaving patch at the hip and a whistle around her neck.

"Good morning," said the lifeguard. "Welcome to the Tadpoles." The Tadpoles were the very beginning swimmers.

"I'm Sandy, and this is my helper, Jeff." Sandy pointed to the older boy. "Okay, let's start by getting into the water."

A few of the kids slipped into the pool. Others stood shyly on the side. Maddie went to the edge and stuck in her toe. Ooh. The water was freezing.

Sandy and Jeff reached for the littlest kids and carried them into the water. Carrie jumped in by herself, holding her nose. Bert ran two steps and did a belly flop.

Show-off, Maddie thought.

Sandy tapped Bert on the shoulder. "What's your name?" she asked him.

"Bert," he said.

"Well, Bert, it looks like you've got a head start on the rest of us. You already know how to put your head under."

"I can dog-paddle, too," said Bert. "But I don't know how to *really* swim."

"Don't worry," said Sandy. "You'll know how very soon."

Carrie was holding on to Jeff's arm, jumping up and down to get warm. Everybody was in the water now. Everybody but Maddie.

Sandy looked at Maddie and asked her her name.

"That's my sister Maddie," Bert said.

Maddie tried to smile.

"Maddie, don't you want to get in with us?" asked Sandy.

"Not really," Maddie said. "It's too cold."

"You'll get used to it," said Sandy. "Come on."

"That's okay," said Maddie. "I'll just stay here and watch."

She sat down on the edge of the pool and let her feet dangle in the water. Jeff bounced toward her, a five-year-old on his arm.

"You shouldn't be scared," Jeff said.

"You're the biggest kid in the group. You should know how to swim by now."

Maddie felt her cheeks get warm. Why did Jeff have to say that?

Maddie knew she was the biggest kid in the group. She knew she should be able to swim already. But she couldn't put her head under water. She just couldn't.

And I never will, Maddie thought. She gritted her teeth. They can't make me. No one can.

Then she remembered the boat trip.

Dad had said that she must pass the beginner test—or she couldn't go on the trip.

He didn't mean it, thought Maddie.

Did he?

5

"So, how was it?" their mother asked as they piled into the car.

"Pretty good," said Carrie. "Sandy is really nice."

"Bob likes Sandy," said Bert.

"Maddie?" asked her mother.

"Okay," Maddie said.

"Maddie didn't go in the water," said Bert.

"Shut up, Bert," said Maddie.

"Why not, Maddie?" asked their mother. "You usually love the pool."

"It's too early in the morning," said Maddie. "It's too cold. And I don't like all the stupid things Sandy makes you do."

"Like what?"

"Like holding on to the side and kicking. It's dumb."

"I like kicking," said Carrie.

"That's because you're a baby," said Maddie.

"I am not!"

"You're all big kids," said their mother. "Especially you, Maddie. You're big enough to learn to swim now. Tomorrow you'll have to get in."

Maddie didn't say anything. She stared out the window at the rows and rows of houses on their way home.

The next morning was a little warmer. Maddie walked slowly down the pool steps into the water.

"It's not so bad once you get in, is it?" Sandy said. She gave Maddie a Styrofoam kickboard. "Just hold on to this and kick," she said. "Soon you'll be zooming all over the pool, just like your brother Bert."

Maddie glanced at Bert, who was playing the penny game with Jeff. Jeff tossed a penny into the pool, and Bert dived down to the bottom and picked it up.

"Bert is just his nickname," Maddie muttered. "His full name is Stupidhead Eggbert."

She took the board from Sandy and started kicking her way across the pool. Carrie had a kickboard, too.

"Let's do bumper cars," Maddie called to her sister. Carrie steered her kickboard straight for Maddie's. The two kickboards bumped, and the girls giggled.

Sandy blew her whistle. "Everybody line up!" she called.

The seven swimming students lined up at the shallow end of the pool. Sandy said, "I think you're all ready for the next step: blowing bubbles."

She divided the children into two groups. Maddie and Carrie were in Jeff's group.

"Let's start with you, Carrie," Jeff said. Jeff stood next to Carrie. "Just close your eyes and put your mouth in the water," he told her. "Now gently blow bubbles out of your mouth."

"What if I swallow some water?" asked Carrie.

"You won't," Jeff said. "Just keep blowing out."

Carrie put her mouth in the water. She blew bubbles.

Maddie felt her stomach knot up. She could hardly stand to watch.

"Okay, Maddie," Jeff said. "Are you ready to try?"

Jeff stood next to Maddie and started telling her what to do. But Maddie could barely hear him. Her eyes locked on the surface of the water.

Her heart was pounding.

The blood rushed to her head.

Her ears were ringing like crazy.

"Help!" Maddie cried. She climbed out of the pool and ran to the dressing room. She locked herself in a bathroom stall.

"I'll never come out," she said.

Maddie shivered. The cement floor of the stall was cold and damp. But the ringing in her ears was gone.

Why do I have to take swimming lessons? she thought. Why, oh, why?

A few minutes later she heard someone coming. Maddie stood on the toilet seat to hide.

"Maddie?" It was Sandy. She knocked on the stall door.

"I know you're in there," she called. "This is the only stall with a locked door."

Maddie frowned. Why hadn't she thought of that?

"Maddie? Don't you feel well?"

"I'm okay," Maddie said.

"Come out," said Sandy. "The lesson is almost over. You don't have to go back in today."

Was it true? Or was it a trap?

"I'm going back to the pool now," Sandy said. "Come out when you're ready."

Maddie heard Sandy's bare feet pad away. She heard the dressing-room door close. It was safe.

Carefully Maddie came out of the stall.

She went to the dressing-room door and
peeked out. The other kids were standing on
the grass with their towels wrapped around
them.

It had not been a trap. The lesson was over.

Whew. That had been a close one.

Maddie began to relax. She didn't have to worry about putting her head under water anymore—until tomorrow.

6

That night Mr. Egg brought home a shopping bag and a big white envelope.

"Guess what I have in here, kids?" he said. He waved the envelope. "Boat pictures!"

"What's in the bag?" asked Maddie. Her father smiled and put the bag on the floor. Maddie and Carrie reached inside and pulled out three strange orange things. They looked kind of like hard pillows covered with straps and buckles.

"What are those?" asked Bert.

"Life jackets," said their father. "In case

you fall in the water, they will help you float.
You'll have to wear them whenever you're
out on deck."

Mr. Egg took one of the life jackets and
put it over Maddie's head. He buckled it and
pulled the straps to tighten it.

"Put mine on!" said Bert.

Maddie helped Bert put on his life jacket.

Her father helped Carrie. Soon all three children were wearing them.

Carrie, Bert, and Maddie gathered around the coffee table. Their father opened the envelope. Inside was a brochure with color pictures of a boat.

"This is just like the boat we'll be sailing on," said Mr. Egg.

He also had a big map of the Chesapeake Bay. It was covered in stiff plastic. One side looked like a normal map, with blue for the water and brown for the land and dots where the towns were. On the other side the map was beige, with squiggly black lines and numbers all over it.

"This is a navigational chart," said Mr. Egg. "That tells us where the water is deep and where it is shallow."

"Just like the pool," said Bert.

Mr. Egg turned the map to the normal side. "Here's where we'll be going on our trip." He traced a route with his finger. "We'll start at Annapolis and sail to Saint Leonard's Creek. Along the way we'll stop in little towns and eat in restaurants."

Maddie loved eating in restaurants. She looked closely at the map, searching for islands. There were lots of them. Big ones and little ones.

She looked at the names on the map. Breezy Point. Point Lookout. Bloodsworth Island.

"Are any of these *desert* islands?" she asked her father.

"I don't know," he said. "We can stop and explore them. Then we'll find out."

Bert studied the boat pictures. "Look at this!" he said. "The table turns into a bed!"

"Let me see," said Maddie. She took the brochure from Bert and looked at the pictures.

There was a cozy nook in the front of the boat where two people could sleep, and another in the back for two more people.

Then there was a picture of the boat's kitchen. It had a tiny sink and narrow cupboards and a table with cushioned benches all around it. Another picture showed a woman flipping the tabletop over to make a bed. It looked so cool.

"I want to sleep on the table," said Bert.

Mrs. Egg came in and said, "Dinner's almost ready."

"What are we having?" Carrie asked.

"Fish," said Mrs. Egg.

"Hey," said their father. "Speaking of fish—how were swimming lessons today?"

"Great!" said Bert. "I'm the best one in the whole class!"

"I put my face in the water and blew bubbles," said Carrie.

Maddie scowled. She hated Bert and Carrie—especially Bert. She hated that they weren't afraid.

"Swimming lessons stink," she said. "I'm not going back."

Maddie saw her father glance at her mother. It was one of those mother-father glances that are supposed to be private but everybody sees them. It annoyed her.

"Well," said Mr. Egg, "you all know the rules. You have to pass the beginner test before you can go on the boat trip."

"You don't really mean it," said Maddie.

"Yes, I do," said her father. "If you don't pass the test you'll have to stay here. Grandma will stay with you."

Maddie watched his face. He didn't smile. He looked serious.

He really means it, she thought. But so do I.

"I don't care," she said. "I won't go on the boat trip. I'll stay here with Grandma and we'll have lots of fun."

Bert stared at Maddie in horror. "Staying with Grandma isn't as good as going sailing," he said.

"It's better," Maddie said. "I can't wait for you all to leave so I can be alone with Grandma. She's going to take me to the store for slushies on hot days. We'll play old maid. She'll let me win every game. We'll go to the movies. We'll make chocolate chip cookies—and I'll get to eat all of them because none of you will be here. I can't wait!"

Bert held out the color brochure. "But Maddie," he said, pointing to the folding kitchen table. "Just look!"

"Who cares?" she shouted. "Who wants

to sleep on a stupid kitchen table? Only a baby like you!"

"Humph!" said Bert. "I'm glad you're not going. You're a big grouch!"

"Maddie, calm down," said her mother.

"No!" Maddie yelled. "I'll never calm down, not ever! I'll never be calm again!"

Maddie ran upstairs to her bedroom and slammed the door.

7

RRRRrrrummmbbblebang!

Wow, thought Maddie. I didn't know I could slam the door so hard.

Crack! Rumble rumble rumble!

That time she hadn't done anything. Maddie glanced out the window. The wind was blowing hard and the sky was turning dark. A thunderstorm was coming.

Too bad it didn't get here this morning, Maddie thought—in time to cancel swimming lessons.

Someone pounded on the bedroom door.

"Maddie! Let me in!" It was Carrie.

"I want to be alone!" said Maddie.

"But I want to get Miss Jackson!" cried Carrie. Miss Jackson was Carrie's doll. "It's my room, too, you know!"

"I don't care. I want my own room!"

Now it sounded as if Carrie were kicking the door. "Maddie!" she screamed.

Let her scream, Maddie thought. She sat on her bed and ignored Carrie.

"Mom!" Carrie screamed. "Maddie locked me out."

"Madison Elizabeth Egg!" shouted her mother. "Open this door right now!"

Crrraaaack! Rumble rumble! More thunder, and this time a flash of lightning.

"Aaaaugh! Mommy!" A wail went through the house. Maddie knew it was Bert screaming. Poor Bert. He was terrified of thunder and lightning. Maddie usually comforted him whenever there was a thunderstorm. She wasn't afraid of storms. She thought they were exciting.

"I'm not afraid of anything," she said to herself.

Except—

"Maddie, I want Miss Jackson!" cried Carrie. "Let me in!"

"Maddie, I'm warning you..." That was her mother speaking.

"Okay, okay," said Maddie. She walked slowly to the door and turned the lock. "Go get your stupid doll. I'll find someplace else to get a little peace and quiet."

Carrie opened the door and marched into the room.

"I hate you," she said to Maddie.

"Good," said Maddie. She left the room, slamming the door behind her again.

"Maddie, that wasn't very nice," said her mother. "But we can talk about it later. Right now I can't find Bert."

There was another flash of lightning, a great crash of thunder, and the rain began to pour down. A piercing scream rang through the house.

"Poor Bert," said Maddie.

"He's somewhere on the second floor," said Mrs. Egg. Then she sniffed the air. "Do I smell something burning?"

Maddie sniffed, too. It *did* smell like something burning.

"The fish!" cried Mrs. Egg. "I forgot all about it!" She ran downstairs to the kitchen.

Another bolt of lightning cut through the sky. *Crash!* went the thunder.

Maddie thought she knew where Bert was. She went to the end of the hall and gently opened the linen closet.

Bert was huddled under the clean towels, shaking.

"Don't be afraid, Bert," said Maddie. "I'm here."

She nestled in next to Bert. There was another flash of lightning, the brightest one yet.

"Shut the door," said Bert. "I don't want the lightning to get me."

"It won't get you," said Maddie, but she shut the door anyway. The linen closet was dark.

"I thought you were scared of the dark," said Maddie.

"It's not as bad as lightning," said Bert. "And it's okay if I'm not alone."

Maddie patted him. "I'm here. But what did you do before I got here?"

"I still wasn't alone," said Bert. "Bob's in here with me. Can't you see him?"

Maddie strained her eyes in the darkness. Then she laughed at herself. How stupid can you get? she thought. I'm trying to see an invisible friend.

But out loud she said, "Hi, Bob. Sorry I didn't see you before."

"Bob's not afraid of anything," Bert said. "Just like you, Maddie."

Maddie was silent for a moment. Then she said, "I'm not so brave."

"Yes, you are," said Bert. "Daddy always calls you Brave Maddie Egg."

"Well," said Maddie. "From now on you can call me Yellow Belly Maddie."

Bert poked her stomach. "Your tummy's not yellow."

Maddie didn't say anything. She just sat with him in the dark for a while. She was thinking about Bert and about being brave.

"Bert," she said. "How do you do it? How do you put your face in the water without being scared?"

"It isn't scary," Bert said. "Why are you scared?"

"I try not to be," said Maddie. "But whenever I try to put my head in the water, I hear this terrible ringing sound. It's so loud I can't think straight! And then I get scared. And then I can't do it."

"You hear ringing?" said Bert. "I know what that is."

Maddie was surprised. "You do?"

"Yeah," said Bert. "It's Bob."

"Bob?"

"He's trying to call you. From his car phone."

Maddie started to laugh, but she knew Bert was serious. Maddie tried to be serious, too. "How can I stop it?" she asked.

"Answer it, silly. Don't you know how to answer the phone?"

Answer it? thought Maddie. Could that really work?

"Bob talks to me when I'm under water," said Bert. "I can hear him better that way. It's nice and quiet under there."

"Bert, you're a nut," said Maddie.

But he was a nut who wasn't afraid of putting his head in the water.

8

Maddie sat in the bathtub after dinner. The thunderstorm was over. The fish had been ruined, so Mr. Egg made bacon, lettuce, and tomato sandwiches for dinner. Maddie didn't mind. She liked BLTs better than fish.

She splashed the water with her hand. It made waves in the tub.

Bert is crazy, she thought. He's a maniac. Whoever heard of an invisible friend named Bob, anyway?

But she kept thinking about Bert sitting in the dark with Bob. And Bob talking to

Bert under water. Bob helped Bert when he was afraid. Could he help Maddie, too?

Just try it, Maddie said to herself. You're all alone. No one can see you. No one will ever know.

She looked at the bathwater. It didn't seem so scary to get her head wet in the tub. It wasn't the same as the pool. What could happen in the bathtub?

Still, she felt her heart begin to pound.

Don't let that stop you, she told herself. Remember, it's only the tub.

She moved her face closer to the water.

Her heart beat faster.

The blood began to rush to her head.

Her ears began to ring.

She put her face to the water. The ringing was getting louder. *Rrriiing!*

Stop it! she thought. No, don't say "Stop it!" Don't panic. Answer it.

Riiing!

Hello? Maddie said in her head. Then she listened hard.

The ringing faded. She kept listening.

She thought she heard a voice.

"Don't be afraid," said the voice.

Was that Bob?

Now the voice said, "You can do it."

Wow, thought Maddie. He's talking to me!

The ringing was gone. Maddie's heart was still pounding, but her head felt clearer. She listened for the voice.

"Just take a deep breath," said Bob. "Then blow out."

She took a deep breath. "Keep going," said Bob.

She let her forehead touch the water. It wasn't so hard with the ringing sound gone. She could think.

She listened for the voice again. "Remember," Bob said. "Don't breathe in. Just blow out."

Maddie pinched her nose closed. Then she let her lips touch the water. She blew out. She made little bubbles.

She did it!

"Try again," said Bob.

Her heart still pounded, but not so hard.
She took a deep breath. She let the water
touch her whole face and her cheeks. She
blew. Out came the bubbles. She was doing
it!

She lifted her face and wiped off the drops of water.

Wow! she thought. I put my whole face in the water! I blew bubbles!

I'm ready, she thought happily. Tomorrow when I go to the pool, I'll be ready to swim!

9

"Ahoy there, matey!" shouted Mr. Egg. He was standing on the deck of a boat that was tied to a dock. Maddie was marching down the dock, carrying a pile of pillows. She was wearing her orange life jacket.

Carrie, Bert, and Mrs. Egg were right behind her. Mr. Egg took the pillows from Maddie. "Is that everything?" he asked.

"Aye, aye, sir," said Maddie.

"Then welcome aboard," said Mr. Egg. "Welcome, my three swimmers. Bert." He lifted Bert off the dock and onto the deck of the boat. "Carrie." He took Carrie's hand

and she jumped aboard. "And last but not least, Brave Maddie Egg, a swimmer if there ever was one."

Maddie smiled and stepped proudly aboard the boat. It was the beginning of August, and swimming lessons were over.

Maddie had passed the Tadpole test with flying colors. She could swim. She could even open her eyes under water.

"Load up the cabin, mateys, and we'll be off!" said Mr. Egg.

Maddie and Carrie took the pillows into the cabin. They put two pillows in the bow, or the front of the boat, where Mr. and Mrs. Egg would be sleeping. They put two pillows in the stern, or the back, where their own bed was.

Bert was going to sleep in the kitchen. But there were two pillows left.

"Why is there an extra pillow?" asked Carrie.

"It's not extra," said Maddie. "It's for Bob." She put it next to Bert's pillow.

Carrie gave Maddie a funny look. "Stop pretending," she said. "Bob isn't real."

"Maybe he is and maybe he isn't," said Maddie.

"Anchors aweigh!" cried Mr. Egg.

The girls went up on deck. Mrs. Egg untied the boat and shoved off. The boat pulled away from the dock and started out into the bay.

Maddie stood by the rail on the bow. She watched the water, holding on tight. She was on the lookout for desert islands.

About the Author

NATALIE STANDIFORD has been writing stories since she was in the third grade. "I decided to write *Brave Maddie Egg*," she says, "because I always had to take swimming lessons as a kid, even though I hated them."

Natalie Standiford is the author of many books for young readers, including *The Bravest Dog Ever: The True Story of Balto* and *The Best Little Monkeys in the World*. She lives in New York City.

About the Illustrator

LYNNE WOODCOCK CRAVATH grew up riding her horse on the wild plains of Montana and considers herself to be "pretty brave about most things." She is the illustrator of several children's books, and her work has appeared in *Ladybug* magazine. She now lives in Arizona with her husband and two children, three dogs, and one very fat cat.